Albert of Saxe-Goth.. ... Good, The Prin... ... fever.

Alfred (The Great, ...) d. 901, aged 52 ... popular acclaim ... the invention o... ... Royal Navy, the ... The Church of ... Restoration of the Muses to Oxford—only pedants dispute this last. Even his weaknesses (culinary neglect and, as a publisher, distressing exploitation of his best selling author, the Venerable Bede) have enduring glamour. Violently pursuing an anti-immigration policy, he fought shattering major battles, Ashdown, Ethendun, Edington and 53 lesser engagements. For 1200 years, he has reigned First in Peace, First in War and First in the Hearts of his Countrymen.

Arthur, son of Geoffrey, Henry II's third son, d. 1202, aged 16, by his Uncle John's contrivance, murdered by drowning in the Seine.

Arthur (of the Round Table, The Once & Future King) b. 498 in several places and still alive, being last seen asleep in a hall beneath Catterick Camp by Potter Thompson, a North Riding man, in 1477.) His principal biographers are Sir Thomas Malorie, Alfred, Lord Tennyson and the English Tourist Authority. However, the only really reliable facts are that he crushed the Saxons in one massive battle at Mount Baden (site unknown by the Ordnance Survey Dept. but confidently and variously plotted by several university professors) and that the distance between the eyes of this enterprising cavalry commander was the span of a man's hand.

Athelstan, son of Edward the Elder's handfast spouse, d. 940, aged 46, raising the minimum age for hanging juvenile delinquents from 12 to 15. His shattering victory over the Danes at Brunaburgh is Britain's most elusive battlefield, sited variously between a Birmingham suburb and Glasgow.

Berstrand, d. 1120, was reported by monks to be the natural son of William Rufus, although they neither named the woman nor brought evidence that Rufus ever lay with one.

Charles I (The Martyr, Saint Charles) d. 1649, aged 49, of decapitation and buried without service. He was slight, of melancholy demeanour and had a severe speech impediment. His admirable personal qualities, deep religious devotion and splendid patronage of painters, were betrayed by an imperfect understanding of many of his subjects' political and religious inclinations.

Charles II (The Merry Monarch), d. 1685 aged 55 of uraemia and mercuric poisoning, a six foot tall, sardonic profligate who maintained a wife, several ladies-in-waiting, a troop of concubines and their numerous progeny. He created a record-breaking 430 baronets and rode several Newmarket winners. Numerous Royal Oak insigns celebrate his hair-raising flight from the Battle of Worcester.

Charles Edward Stuart (Charles III, Bonnie Prince Charlie, The Young Pretender, Betty Burke) d. 1789, aged 66, in Rome. During his legendary 14 month Scottish campaign and flight he was tall and slim, with a sharp chin, large mouth and lustreless blue eyes. In later life, he deteriorated into a wife-batterer and a querulous drunk.

Cnut, d. 1053, a Danish progressive, who disestablished the Norse gods and substituted the title 'jarl' (earl) for 'ealderman'. A confrontation with the Solent tide urged on him by his public relations advisors is the 3rd best remembered event in English history.

Cole (Old King Cole).

Cunobelinus, the British King of Hertfordshire, immortalised as Cymbeline by Wm. Shakespeare.

Cynewulf, King of Wessex, d. 754 whilst entertaining a young woman from Merton.

Edgar the Atheling, d. 1120, aged 60, son of Edward the Exile and grandson of Edmund Ironside, was named King by the archbishops after Harold's death at Hastings. Too timorous a soul to accept this dubious honour, he fled and died naturally.

Edgar the Peaceful, d. 975, aged 32, a handsome dwarf, who demonstrated his overlordship by having eight sub-kings row him up and down the Dee. His anti-crime measures (nostril-slitting, eye-gouging and ear-ripping) were horrifyingly effective. When an Andover ealderman, invited to provide his daughter as the royal guest's bedmate, substituted a housemaid, this poor girl, having given every satisfaction, was awarded her employer and his family as servants.

Edmund I, d. 946, aged 26, from stabbing whilst arresting an uninvited outlaw at a feast at Pucklekirk (Glos.).

Edmund, eldest son of Harold II, fled to Ireland in 1066.

Edmund, King of East Anglia, d. 869 from execution by arrow-shots when, after the battle of Hoxne, he fell into Danish hands. His memorials are Bury St. Edmunds and a wall painting at Pickering.

Edmund Ironside, d. 1016 aged 23 and buried at Glastonbury. He was an exceptionally strong and resolute young man and, but for his death by assassination, might have solved the Danish immigrant problem.

Edmund Mortimer, 5th Earl of March, d. 1425, aged 34, great-grandson of Edward III. Profiting from the fate of his father who fatally joined the Percy-Hotspur Rebellion, he did not pursue a claim, remained faithful to Henry IV and died in his service in Ireland.

Edred, d. 955, aged 30, from a bludgeoning by the Norseman, Eric Bloodaxe. Even before this traumatic experience, his digestive organs were so disordered that dinner guests watched in fascinated horror as he first masticated food, then noisily sucked in its juices and, finally, spat out the residue.

Edward I, (Longshanks, Malleus Scotorum) d. 1307 aged 67, of a violent flux. He was unusually tall and had curly hair, sparkling black eyes, one drooping eyelid and a stammer. His first wife, Eleanor of Castile, bore 15 children and inspired an astonishing progress of memorial crosses, built whilst he was enjoying a second wife, 42 years his junior. This choleric man banished the Jews, planned several new towns, stole the Stone of Scone, subdued Wales and, at death's approach, still consumed with a lifelong antipathy against Scotsmen ordered that, after his heart had been despatched to Jerusalem, his bones must be borne before an invading army.

Edward II (Edward of Caernarvon), d. 1327 aged 43, was a handsome, affable man who, failing to fulfil the expectations of his excessively amorous wife, was discarded and murdered in Berkeley Castle (Glos.) by having a red-hot wire thrust into his entrails through a horn tube.

Edward III, d. 1377 aged 65 of shingles, the most handsome Plantagenet, a selfish and, later, lethargic, self-indulgent man. Invoking Salic Law he initiated the bloody, wasteful Hundred Years War. He is said to have coined that most unanswerable of moral disclaimers, *Honi soit qui mal y pense.* Before leaving the world, he had the mortification of seeing the world leave him.

Edward IV, d. 1483 aged 42, of a surfeit. This splendidly corpulent giant, then Duke of York, usurped the Crown by victories at Towton (Yorks), Northampton and Mortimer's Cross (Hereford). He maintained a talented seraglio and abolished truck payments of pins to garment trade workers.

Edward V (The Prince in the Tower), d. 1483, aged 13, by smothering. His bones were unearthed in 1680 and re-examined in 1933.

Edward VI, only legitimate son of Henry VIII, d. 1553, aged 15, of tuberculosis.

Edward VII, d. 1910 aged 69 of bronchitis, was a short, tubby and usually affable man whose favourite pastimes were the pursuit of gamebirds and handsome, amply-built women.

Edward VIII, (The Duke of Windsor) d. 1972 aged 78 of throat cancer. He reigned 325 days and never was crowned, abdicating to become the third husband of Mrs. Simpson, an American.

Edward the Confessor, d. 1060, aged 62, was a gentle albino who, to conceal his own inadequacy, pettishly imprisoned his wife. He established a great reputation as a faith-healer by allowing scrofula (King's evil) patients to touch his person. The foundation of Westminster Abbey is his enduring memorial.

Edward the Elder, d. 924 at Farndon-on-Dee, for a quarter-century an outstanding commander in the Danish Immigrant Wars. He married twice and also maintained a beautiful shepherdess who, having dreamed that the moon shone from her womb, bore Athelstan.

Edward the Martyr, d. 978 aged 16 at Corfe, at the instigation of his step-mother, stabbed whilst drinking a stirrup-cup.

Edmund Seymour, Duke of Somerset and Protector of the Realm, executed 1552, aged 46. He was a refined, sensitive man with a true love of liberty and affection for the poor.

Edward, Earl of Warwick, nephew of Edward IV, who, until his execution in 1499 by Henry VII, had a reasonable claim to the crown.

Edward of Woodstock (The Black Prince), d. 1376 aged 46, of dysentery, was a gifted army commander employed by his father, Edward III, to devastate France. He was a notorious gambler and married his cousin as her third husband. He purloined the insignia of Three Feathers from the blind King of Bohemia, killed at Crecy. His armour hangs above his tomb in Canterbury Cathedral.

Edwin, King of Northumbria, d. 633 aged 48, in battle near Doncaster against the Pagan, Penda of Mercia. Earlier he had erased one of the last surviving Celtic kingdoms, Elmet in Yorkshire.

Edwy the All-fair, d. 959, aged 19 of excess. The coronation of this youthful satyr was delayed whilst the Archbishop of Canterbury dislodged him from bed where he was lying between his voluptuous sweetheart and her equally amorous mother.

Egbert, d. 839, ended the Heptarchy (Essex, Sussex, Kent, Mercia, E. Anglia, Northumbria, Wessex) when he was reluctantly acknowledged 1st King of England. He pacified Cornwall and forbade any Welshman on pain of death to cross Offa's Dyke.

Egfrid, Bretwalda of Northumbria, d. 684 aged 40, was the island's most disastrous general, losing one army in Ireland and another in a Scots bog.

Ella, Bretwalda of Northumbria had the Viking, Ragnar Lodbrok, cast into a snake-pit from which (unlike numerous silent movies) no-one rescued him.

Ella, 1st King of Sussex. I can provide no further information other than that I had an aunt named after him.

Ethelbald, d. 860, pursued an energetic anti-Danish immigrant policy. He married his 15 year old step-mother.

Ethelbert, Ethelbald's brother, d. 866, also bloodily engrossed with the Danish immigrant problem.

Ethelbert, King of Kent, d. 616, whose wife, Bertha, introduced Augustine the Missionary into the country.

Ethelred the Saint, d. 871 in battle at Merton, his sixth in a year. He is buried at Sherborne.

Ethelred the Unready (The Redeless, the Exile) d. 1016, aged 48. This shiftless, erratic and treacherous man, his treasury emptied of appeasing Danegeld, enlisted racial prejudice, inflamed by the immigrants' success with English women (because of their more frequent baths). The resulting St. Brice's Day Massacre awoke massive Danish retaliation: he fled to the Continent and died there.

Ethelwulf, d. 856, a sluggish uxorious man much addicted to religious practices, who, aged 58 and against the advice of St. Dunstan and his physicians, married Charlemagne's 13 year old grand-daughter. One of his natural sons became a popular Oxford don.

Frederick Louis, eldest son of George II, whose mock epitaph reads:

> Here lies Fred,
> Who was alive and is dead,
> There's no more to be said.

George I, first Hanoverian king, d. 1727 aged 67 of a coronary thrombosis, based his claim on descent from James I's daughter, Elizabeth of Bohemia. Refusing to learn English, he argued with his ministers in French and dog-Latin. Suspecting her adultery, he imprisoned his wife for life and took on two huge German mistresses, known to Londoners as the Elephant and Castle.

George II, d. 1760, aged 77 of a stroke (whilst in the water-closet). He was a snorer on the grand scale, a fantastically exacting time-keeper (who even insisted that his mistresses came promptly), was the last king to lead an army into battle (at Dettingen) and, when urged by his dying wife to remarry, sobbed, 'Non, j'aurai des maitresses.'

George III, d. 1820, aged 82, of senility, after long affliction by porphyria, contemporaneously diagnosed as royal-flying-gout (madness). Domestically, he was exemplary; all his 15 children were his wife's too.

George IV (The Prince Regent, The First Gentleman, Prinny) d. 1830, aged 68, of a stomach rupture and alcoholic cirrhosis. He married secretly a beautiful widow, Mrs. Fitzherbert, and then, bigamously, Caroline of Brunswick who mistreated scandalously. To pay for his inspired patronage of the arts and vices he borrowed heavily and his I.O.U.'s were bought and sold like government securities.

George V, 2nd son of Edward VII, d. 1936, aged 71, of bronchitis.

George VI, d. 1952, aged 56, of lung cancer, succeeded after his elder brother's abdication and built the monarchy to a peak of popularity.

George, Duke of Clarence, d. 1479, aged 28, drowned in a butt of malmsey and buried at Tewkesbury, was a younger brother of Edward IV.

George, Prince of Denmark, Queen Anne's husband, d. 1708, aged 55. This overweight, amiable and virile glutton fathered 18 children, none surviving infancy.

Hardicnut, d. 1042, aged 22 (whilst proposing the bride's health at a wedding breakfast, having earlier had his predecessor's body dug up, beheaded and flung into a bog).

Harold II, the last Saxon king, d. 1066, aged 44, of an arrow wound and multiple stabs and buried at Waltham Abbey. He was a tall, temperate man and an energetic commander.

Harold Harefoot, d. 1040 aged 23. He had unusually hairy legs, was Hardicnut's half-brother, was crowned at Oxford and buried at Winchester.

Henry I (Beauclerk) d. 1135 aged 65 of a surfeit of lampreys and buried at Reading. He was so tall that he walked across the Thames and so virile that he holds the royal record for propagation—24 undisputed offspring. Even so, after the Wreck of the White Ship, his sole legal heir was a daughter. The stench of this Yorkshireman's corpse was so offensive that, before it was coated with salt and parcelled in ox-hide, an embalmer collapsed and died.

Henry II (Curtmantle, Fitzempress) d. 1189 aged 56 of a fever and buried at Fontevraud. This unusually able, energetic and choleric man (the first Plantagenet) had a large spherical head, close-cropped reddish hair, grey bloodshot eyes, a cracked voice and legs bruised livid from hard riding. To purge his guilty complicity in the a-Becket murder he let himself be scourged by 70 Canterbury monks. When his lately rebellious son visited to view his corpse, blood gushed from its nose until Richard left the room. So they say.

Henry III, d. 1272 aged 66 of a languishing distemper and partly buried in a gold cup at Westminster. He was of moderately compact build, had a furrowed brow, one drooping eyelid and normally conversed in French. He claimed that fining rebels was more profitable than hanging them, established a primitive consumer protection service, built a small house for converted Jews and enlarged the prosperity of barristers by abolishing Trial by Fire & Water.

Henry IV (Bolingbroke) d. 1413 aged 47 of either leprosy, postulated eczema, gout or an apoplectic fit. This usurper was a shortish compact man with good teeth for his times and a russet beard. He survived several plots including a proposal to embed him on nails. He swore that he would die in Jerusalem and in the Jerusalem Chamber at Westminster he died.

Henry V (of Monmouth) d. 1422, aged 35, of dysentery, pleurisy, piles or a flux, though some say of St. Anthony's Fire. This oval faced, bright eyed Victor of Agincourt (wrongly believed to closely resemble Sir Laurence Olivier) declared on his deathbed that he would wrest Jerusalem from the infidels.

Henry VI, d. 1461 aged 50, of either stabbing or melancholia, was so naive that some unkindly allege imbecility, so chaste that even a hint of a cleavage caused him to explaim 'Fie!', so devout that, even aged 3, he howled and screamed at suggested Sabbath Day travel, so sexually modest that, when his fierce French wife bore an heir, he declared that the father must have been the Holy Ghost. Nevertheless, he is the undisputed progenitor of Eton and King's, Cambridge.

Henry VII, d. 1509, aged 52, of either rheumatoid arthritis or gout which turned ptific. This cheerful-faced but unamiable Welsh miser with rotting teeth, employing Morton's Fork, left £2,000,000 (their money). He organized a formidable European spy ring and built a magnificent chapel at Westminster.

Henry VIII, d. 1547, aged 55, of chronic sinusitis complicated by peritonitis of the leg and syphilis. When young, this red-haired monster was personable, athletic, artistically creative and vicious. Later, he grew corpulent, pig-eyed, moved in an aura of repulsively putrefying stench and stayed vicious. He debased the coinage, cowed the nobility, judiciously murdered two wives and was still issuing death-warrants on his deathbed.

Henry Benedict Maria Clement (Henry IX, Cardinal York) d. 1807 aged 82. This grandson of James II bequeathed the Stuart crown jewels to George IV whose father had helped him out with a pension.

Henry, Duke of Buckingham, great-grandson of Edward III and leader of the Old Nobility, executed 1483 at Shrewsbury. A phenomenal Severn flood dispersed his Welsh army and he was betrayed by an ingrate.

Henry Fitzroy, d. 1536 aged 17, born at Jericho (Essex), son of Liz Blount and Henry VIII who showered titles upon him and whose secret heir he may have been.

Henry, 3rd Earl of Huntingdon, great-great grandson of Edward IV's brother did not pursue his claim.

Henry Pole, Lord Montagu, elder son of Edward IV's niece Margaret, had a reasonable claim until his execution in 1538.

James I (James VI of Scotland, Wisest Fool in Christendom) d. 1625, aged 62, of either Bright's Disease or a tertian ague brought on by fits. He was small with spindly legs, stuttered, slavered at meals and had homosexual inclinations. His early home life was intolerable—his mother married his father's murderer and, later, was herself judicially murdered. At a going-rate of £1,000-£2,000 (cash down) he dubbed 237 knights on his way south from Scotland, 300 at his coronation and, despite the danger (two or three aspirants were poked in the eye by the dubbing sword) continued to attract eager customers.

James II (Tom Otter) d. 1688 aged 68 of a cerebral haemorrhage and buried at St. Germains. He was a brave, stubborn and swarthy man who misunderstood the mood of his countrymen. Besides a second wife of 15, he kept numerous plain mistresses who, after his conversion to popery, were explained by his brother, Charles, as penances imposed by priests.

James Edward Stuart (James III, The Old Pretender, Chevalier St. George) d. 1760, aged 78, widely believed to have been a suppositious baby borne in a warming-pan. This lanky son of James II and Mary of Modena looked cheerful without feeling merry. In exile, he had particular consolation from watching his image being struck on medals.

James, Duke of Monmouth and Buccleuch (Mr. Fitzroy, Mr. Cork) d. 1685, aged 36, by execution and buried without service. This son of Charles II and the 'beautiful, brown, bold but insipid' Lucy Walters of Haverford-west, deserted his supporters at Sedgemoor, was un-earthed from a New Forest ditch and grovelled for mercy before his uncle. So that a portrait commission might be fulfilled, his head (which 'took four choppes') was sewn back on.

John (Lackland) d. 1216, aged 50, at Newark from dysentery aggravated by the vexatious loss of his treasury in The Wash. During fits of dejection he gnawed straws and small sticks. A post-mortem in 1797 at Worcester revealed that he had been 5 foot tall and that his last meal (at Swineshead) was peaches and new cider. I quite admire him—he bought books instead of borrow-ing them.

John Dudley, Earl of Warwick, Duke of Northumberland, Protector, d. 1553, aged 51, on the block. He was a bad man on the make and is the only character in English History for whom no-one has put in a good word.

Maudlin d. 1400 of fright, was Richard II's double and set up as a pretender by an assortment of nobles and bishops. Having set Cirencester afire, the rebels were put down by its furious Mayor and ratepayers who, off their own bats, there and then beheaded the Earls of Salisbury and Surrey as an example to the rest.

Offa, Bretwalda of Mercia, d. 796, now remembered for his prodigious Dyke but, contemporaneously, celebrated as a marriage-broker, failing only with the daughters of Charlemagne who preferred them to sin at home than marry abroad.

Oliver Cromwell (King Noll), Lord Protector, d. aged 59 of a tertian ague, in 1658, during a tremendous storm on September 3rd, anniversary of his victories at Dunbar and Worcester. This red-haired Cambridge graduate of partly Welsh descent and of Puritanical inclination, a man of great force of character, at the age of 41 discovered himself to be a military genius. Although a prime mover of an astonishing rebellion, by temperament he was a conservative and, at times, a savage one. After the Restoration his body was dug up and hung at Tyburn. His mummified head for many years was stored in an East Anglian parson's hat-box.

Osbert, Bretwalda of Northumbria, d. 867, whilst ousting the Danes from York, having lost much support by raping his coastal commander's wife.

Oswald of Northumbria, d. 642, in battle at Oswestry. Earlier, against the odds, he had defeated and slain Penda, the notorious pagan. Until it was stolen from Bamburgh Church, his severed hand was a sovereign remedy for manifold ailments.

Penda, Bretwalda of Mercia, d. 655, aged 78, in battle at Winwood, a Leeds suburb, claimed direct descent from Woden.

Philip, Queen Mary's consort (Philip II of Spain) d. 1598 aged 71 of general corporeal corruption.

Reginald, Cardinal Pole, 2nd son of Edward IV's niece Margaret, d. 1558, did not pursue a tenuous claim to the crown.

A simple guide through the maze for foreigners with good eyesight.

Saxon

* When in distress, follow thick lines and the numbers.

1. Egbert — Ethelwulf 2

Ethelbald 3 — Ethelbert 4 — Ethelred 5 — Ethelswith — Alfred 6

Aethelflaed, Lady of Mercia — Edward the Elder 7 — Ethelgifu, Abbess of Shaftesbury — Aelfthryth Ethelweard
8 Athelstan 9 Edmund i Edred Edgyth Edgifu (m. Charles the Simple)
Edwig
Edward the Martyr 12 Ethelflaed Edgar 13 m. Elfthryth
Edmund Ironside 14 Athelstan Edwig Alfred Athelred ii 15 m. Emma m. Cnut
Edward the Exile Goda Harold H
Edgar the Atheling St. Margaret m. Malcolm iii of Scotland Edward the Confessor 18 Harthacnut 17

Danes

Harold 19 Godwinson

William i 20 **Norman**

Robert 21 William ii 22 Henry i Adela m. Stephen of Blois
William Matilda 23 m. Henry i 24 Stephen Henry of Blois
Eleanor of Aquitaine m. Henry ii 24 Eustace William
Henry Matilda m. Henry the Lion Richard i 25 Geoffrey John 26

Plantagenet

Arthur
27 Richard of Cornwall Joanna m. K of Scots Isabel Eleanor m. Simon de Montfort
Henry iii
28 Edward i Margaret m. K of Scots Beatrice Edmund E of Lancaster
29 Edward ii Edmund, E of Kent Thomas Henry
30 Edward iii Joan, Fair Maid of Kent m. the Black Prince Edmund of Langley
Edward the Black Prince Lionel of Clarence John of Gaunt
31 Richard ii Philippa Henry iv 32 John Beaufort
Roger Mortimer John
Anne Mortimer Henry v 33 Marg. m. Edmund Tudor

Lancaster

Richard of York m. Cicely Nevil Henry vi 34

York

35 Edward iv m. Margaret George of Clarence Richard iii 37 Henry vii (Tudor) 38
36 Edward v Richard

Arthur m. Catharine m. Henry viii 39 Mary Margaret m. James iv of Scotland
Mary 41 Elizabeth 42 Edward vi 40 James
Mary Q of Scots

Tudor

Stuart

Henry Charles i 44 Elizabeth m. Frederick Elector Palatine
45 Charles ii Mary James ii 44 Charles Rupert Sophia m. Elector Hanover
48 William iii m. Mary Anne 44 James George i 50
We publish a dictionary Charles Edward Henry George ii 51
of Unseen Queens. and so on

Hanover

Richard I (Coeur de Lion) d. 1199 aged 42 from a direct hit by a frying pan fired by a French cross-bowman whilst enforcing a claim to a valuable archeological find. He had auburn hair, furiously blue eyes and apelike arms. His body was buried at his father's feet at Fontevraud, his heart at Rouen and his bowels at Poitiers.

Richard II (of Bordeaux) d. 1400, aged 32, at Pomfret from either starvation, neurasthenia or, whilst defending himself with a poleaxe, from stabbing by a man stood on a chair. The first royal portrait painted contemporaneously depicts a fresh faced, fair-haired dandy. Until his jawbone was stolen in 1776 by a juvenile delinquent (whose family hid it until 1900), tourists were permitted to touch his head through a hole in his Westminster tomb.

Richard III (Crouchback) d. 1485, aged 33, of wounds, near a thorn bush on Bosworth Field, and buried in Leicester where, later, his coffin was converted into a trough at the White Horse Inn. Details of his appearance differ wildly, some declaring that, after two years in the womb, he emerged with teeth to grow into a hairy hunchback with a withered arm; others that he was elegant but on the small side. Wm. Shakespeare cast him as a stage villain and saddled him with his most parodied line. Readers of the Times will be pleased to hear that he wrote one of the earliest letters urging the suppression of Vice.

Robert, Duke of Normandy (Curt-hose), the Conqueror's eldest son, a short, fat, chatty man, d. 1135, of chagrin, at being sent a cast-off mantle by his youngest brother who had imprisoned him for 26 years in Cardiff Castle.

Richard Cromwell (Tumbledown Dick), Lord Protector, d. 1712 aged 86. This discreet man retired with a golden handshake after a single uncomfortable year in office, living first in Switzerland and, finally, in Cheshunt.

Robert, Earl of Gloucester, eldest bastard of Henry I, d. 1147, of a fever. His mother was Nesta, daughter of Rhys, Prince of South Wales. He was loyal to his step-sister, Matilda.

Richard Neville, Earl of Warwick, (the Kingmaker) d. 1471 of wounds at the Battle of Barnet. He had been entrusted with the care of his infant son by the dying Henry V.

Richard, Duke of York, smothered in the Tower of London, 1483, aged 9. The two princes' bones were found beneath a stair in 1680 and reburied in an urn at Westminster.

Sigeburt, Bretwalda of E. Anglia, d. 644, whilst, knowing it to be God's wish, advancing on the pagan Mercians armed only with a switch.

Lambert Simnel, d. 1525, aged 50, an Oxford organ-builder's son, promoted by a parson as the younger Prince in the Tower. When his credulous Irish supporters were scattered at Stoke-on-Trent, he gave such satisfactory service as a scullion in the royal kitchen that he was made a falconer and died naturally.

Simon de Montfort, Regent, d. 1265 aged 57. After the Battle of Evesham this formidable Frenchman's corpse was stripped down to its hair-shirt and flung into a river.

Stephen, d. 1154, aged 50, of either a heart attack or colic and piles and buried at Faversham in the river. The disputed reign of this fairly likeable great-nephew of William I was so catastrophic that it was despairingly supposed that Christ and the Saints slept.

Sweyn Forkbeard, d. 1014, of apoplexy at Bury St. Edmunds. This bloodthirsty Dane compelled the Witan to elect him after his ejection of Ethelred the Unready.

Thomas, Lord Stafford, great-grandson of Edward IV's brother, might be said to have had a tenuous claim until his execution in 1557.

Perkin Warbeck, d. 1449, aged 25, a Tournai impersonator of the younger Prince in the Tower, who, after deserting two invading bands of his supporters and escaping thrice from jail, was hung.

William I (The Conqueror, The Bastard) d. 1087, aged 60, from abdominal rupture when his rearing horse jerked him into his saddle pummel. This shrewd, ruthless, red-haired natural son of Robert the Devil and a tanner's daughter, ruled with a rod of iron, allocating the defeated Saxon landowners a mere one-eighth of their former possessions. His funeral being delayed by a dissatisfied litigant, the body burst from its too constricted coffin.

William II (Rufus) d. 1100 aged 44 from a mysterious bow-shot whilst hunting. He was florid, tubby, yellow-haired, had eyes of different colour and an unusually loud stammer. His reign having been punctuated by natural disasters—(the 1089 Earthquake, several comets or UFO's, the Finchamsted blood-spring, the drowning of the Goodwin Sands)—satisfyingly culminated in the collapse of Winchester Cathedral roof upon his tomb.

William III (of Orange, Stinking Billy) d. 1702, aged 53, from complications caused by a fractured collar-bone when his horse tripped over a molehill. This asthmatic, hook-nosed resolute Dutchman, Charles I's nephew, facially disfigured by smallpox, suffered the English with wry patience. It is said that his grief at the death of his wife, Mary, was frightening and, until death, he wore a black ribbon secured by a lock of her hair.

William IV (The Sailor King), brother of George IV, d. 1837 aged 72, was an embarrassingly candid man.

William, Earl of Boulogne, d. 1160, without issue. He was King Stephen's son but was loyal to Henry II.

Vortigern, d. 485 in a blazing Welsh castle. This Ancient British king, fatally employing one batch of Baltic immigrants to eject another, lost his kingdom, his life and his honour—this last by the barter of Kent for Hengist and Horsa's pulchritudinous blonde niece.